*indigo*mania

truth serum *vol.* 4

First published as a collection March 2020
Content copyright © Truth Serum Press and individual authors
Edited by Matt Potter

BP#00087

All rights reserved by the authors and publisher. Except for brief excerpts used for review or scholarly purposes, no part of this book may be reproduced in any manner whatsoever without express written consent of the publisher or the author/s.

Truth Serum Press
32 Meredith Street
Sefton Park SA 5083
Australia

Email: truthserumpress@live.com.au
Website: https://truthserumpress.net/
Store: https://truthserumpress.net/catalogue/

Cover design copyright © Matt Potter

ISBN: 978-1-925536-03-4

Also available as an eBook
ISBN: 978-1-925536-84-3

A note on differences in punctuation and spelling:
Truth Serum Press proudly features writers from all over the English-speaking world. Some speak and write English as their first language, while for others, it's their second or third or even fourth language. Naturally, across all versions of English, there are differences in punctuation and spelling, and even in meaning. These differences are reflected in the work *Truth Serum Press* publishes, and they account for any differences in punctuation, spelling and meaning found within these pages.

Truth Serum Press is a member of the
Bequem Publishing collective
http://www.bequempublishing.com/

The term "indigomania" was coined for the Impressionists' "unhealthy" passion for blues.

from ***The essence of blue***
by Belinda Recio and Catherine Kouts

The term *indigomania*, for example, which critics used to describe Impressionists' seemingly irrational passion for blues and violets, not only carried with it certain psychological and medical implications – Huysmans originally described Impressionists' indigomania as a bizarre form of color blindness brought on by mental illness – but also referenced the culture of intense, short-lived fads ... Indigomania was not so much a physiological phenomenon as a social and economic one born of modern consumer culture.

... "One year one paints violet and people scream, and the following year every one paints a great deal of violet," Manet remarked on a different occasion.

from ***Color in the Age of Impressionism: Commerce, Technology, and Art***
by Laura Anne Kalba

· Allen ASHLEY · Linda BARRETT ·
· Claudia BIERSCHENK · Henry BLADON · John BOST ·
· Howard BROWN · Gretel BULL · William BUTLER ·
· Bernise CAROLINO · Chuka Susan CHESNEY ·
· Jan CHRONISTER · Beverly M. COLLINS ·
· Michael T. COOLEN · Linda M. CRATE ·
· Al DeGENOVA · Ruth Z. DEMING · Alyson FAYE ·
· Alan FYFE · Audri GASKINS · Howie GOOD ·
· Ken GOSSE · Samuel GULLIKSSON · Mike HALL ·
· David B. HAMILTON · Ilona HEGEDUS ·
· Ryn HOLMES · Matthew HORSFALL ·
· Sharron HOUGH · Mark HUDSON · Doug JACQUIER ·
· Joanne JAGODA · Mera Baid KAUR ·
· Mary Anna KRUCH · Ann Neuser LEDERER ·
· Josh LEFKOWITZ · Cynthia LESLIE-BOLE ·
· Karen LOUISE · Jan McCARTHY ·
· Charlotte McCORMAC · Jay McPHERSON ·
· Karla Linn MERRIFIELD · Corey MESLER ·
· April MILLER · Marsha MITTMAN · Wilda MORRIS ·
· Colleen MOYNE · Mark A. MURPHY ·
· Remngton MURPHY · Piet NIEUWLAND ·
· Carl 'Papa' PALMER · Tim PHILIPPART ·
· Winston PLOWES · Brad ROSE ·
· Ruth Sabath ROSENTHAL · Ed RUZICKA ·
· Kathryn SADAKIERSKI · Rosie SANDLER ·
· Gerard SARNAT · Mir-Yashar SEYEDBAGHERI ·
· Samara SHAW · Lucy TYRRELL ·
· Patricia UNSWORTH · Jill VANCE · Terry WHITE ·
· Allan J. WILLS · Lynn WOOLLACOTT ·
· Mantz YORKE ·

1   Eavesdropping at the Algonquin Blue Bar
    Karla Linn Merrifield

3   Sickness unto Death
    Howie Good

4   What I Like
    Ed Ruzicka

6   Synergamillion
    David B. Hamilton

8   As_2O_5
    Henry Bladon

9   Please Turn on the Light
    Sharron Hough

10 Iris Blue
    Ruth Sabath Rosenthal

12 Tassels and Silks
    Tim Philippart

13 Royal
    Audri Gaskins

14 God Might be a Potato
    Al DeGenova

16 The Last Decent Man
    Corey Mesler

17 Fragile Mineral Rights
    Piet Nieuwland

18	Reflections	
	Doug Jacquier	
20	John and Mary Sing the Blues	
	Jan McCarthy	
22	Song of Summer Night	
	Mir-Yashir Seyedbagheri	
24	Blue mackerel	
	Allan J. Wills	
26	Out of the Blue	
	Charlotte McCormac	
27	Midday Sky	
	Beverly M. Collins	
28	Claustrophobia	
	Rosie Sandler	
30	Big Sea	
	Alan Fyfe	
31	Life Imitates Art	
	Colleen Moyne	
32	Dawn	
	Karen Louise	
33	Betta Fish	
	Jay McPherson	
34	Half-Life	
	Winston Plowes	

35	The Blue Fields	*Patricia Unsworth*
36	Blue Kisses	*Alyson Faye*
38	Blue Evening	*Wilda Morris*
39	Scarcity Blessing	*Ann Neuser Lederer*
40	The Novice	*Cynthia Leslie-Bole*
43	The Notebook	*Ilona Hegedus*
44	Green on Blue	*Mantz Yorke*
46	Childhood Toys	*Carl 'Papa' Palmer*
47	The Less Busy Season	*Josh Lefkowitz*
48	Mediocrity	*Samuel Gulliksson*
49	In my house, a conspiracy	*Mera Baid Kaur*
50	blue beaches	*Bernise Carolino*

52   Ye Olde Gaol Cell
       Ruth Z. Deming

53   I wish you were awake, Luther
       Claudia Bierschenk

54   Where I Walk in Denali
       Lucy Tyrrell

56   The Alice-Blue Nightie of Sweet Aphrodite
       Ken Gosse

60   Color of Paint
       Jan Chronister

61   Walking In, Walking Out
       Mark A. Murphy

62   Doesn't anybody make blue movies anymore?
       Allen Ashley

63   off-colour
       Jill Vance

64   Blue Period
       Linda Barrett

65   Blue
       April Miller

66   Layers of Blue
       Kathryn Sadakierski

68   Gramercy, All Hallows Eve
       Terry White

70   Gift
            Mary Anna Kruch

72   Blue Sky Piggy Blimp Kamikaze
            Gerard Sarnat

74   To make carbon of diamonds
            Gretel Bull

77   Nursing home visit, with cornflowers
            Lynn Woollacott

78   An Angel in a Blue Prius
            Joanne Jagoda

80   A Bunch of Things god Doesn't Deserve
            Michael J. Coolen

84   Variations in the Perception of Color
            Howard Brown

86   Airport Interlude
            Marsha Mittman

87   Sky is the Dream of Trees
            Brad Rose

88   On the island again
            John Bost

90   How Can You Say That?
            William Butler

91   Fringe Dwellers' Sonnet
            Matthew Horsfall

92	Back in the Blue	
	Mike Hall	
94	A Study in Indigo	
	Remngton Murphy	
96	Bluesville	
	Ryn Holmes	
97	It's a hard word	
	Samara Shaw	
98	Blueberries versus Sausages	
	Mark Hudson	
100	Forbidden Shower	
	Susan Chuka Chesney	
102	Break Open Your Eyes	
	Linda M. Crate	

Eavesdropping at the Algonquin Blue Bar

Karla Linn Merrifield

He's elbowed up, back to me; but over his left shoulder
I can study the woman who keeps taking deep breaths,

grinning, giggling, fingering her hair between martini sips.
She seems to be pinking up in her cheeks.

I watch her wiggling on the leather bar-chair seat
when her consort, in small increments, eases

first two, three inches closer between her thighs,
to which she thrice taps his chest emphatically.

I have…a few goodies…for you, she coyly says.
I bet you do, winks he, and then she—effervesces:

*Rest assured, indeed, that…too…will be! But I mean, I mean—
books, poet pal. Our books, boyo. Plural books!*

Read me yours; I'll read you mine; read each other's!
In bed! King-sized! For poetry…oh…so…fucking…hot!

The man shakes his head, slips his left hand, deftly I must say,
beneath her sassy skirt, and smothers her gasp with his mouth—

in a kiss that is, I'm convinced, destined, rest-assured, indeed,
to go down in The Algonquin's thick tome of literary history.

~ Clive, Bartender, Landmark Fixture

Sickness unto Death

Howie Good

I pulled up my shirt to show the doctor the painful rash that had appeared like stigmata on my front and back. He looked at it, then shrugged. "What do you think it is?" he asked. I decided at that moment to stop carrying my phone everywhere. Somehow disturbing news still managed to reach me. I was out of step with the times. My days were endless. I walked on the beach, took naps, tried to teach myself the guitar. There was a blue iris sitting in a bottle on my table. It would have made a lovely Hallmark card.

What I Like

Ed Ruzicka

That instant when nerves fire,
flare to muscle shovel blade
out from muck's suction

and all comes up mad with facets flashing.
Rain's slivers, crumbled foil, lead
all shine in the shovel full.
Fast streams, mounds, beads.

Sludge fades back to
black and dun
by the time I get it
slopped out,
sloping down a pile.

Down in the hole,
three quick ticks only
before earth's pail-full of blue
regathers. Shoots intense
as a glance from a kid's eye.
That much fire of azure expanse
reflects, restful. Back to
what it was, walled by clay.

That is when a near-by dove
sends its cool grotto of a coo over me.
So I rest, still, elbow atop the shovel.

I lean the bird's way
for a few spasms
of my gurgling heart.

The coolness of wet dirt
on palm and fingers
as I massage bush roots in.
Muscle work. Just that
and that and that.
I could go for some of that; I could be
the king of the world on only the tiniest bit.
I could be in heaven if I could only have
the merest fraction of what he's got;
one day like his day, once or twice a year.

If only, if only, if only.

Synergamillion

David B. Hamilton

So you're driving down the road thinking of Marianne
Moore and wondering why when an Edsel
Passes you gliding the other way.
You're in a restaurant, pausing over coq au vin
On the menu, and though you pass it up
Surprise yourself by asking for a cocoa for dessert.
Or that time hiking in Joshua Tree Park
When you started humming the tune
Of him who fit the battle of Jericho.
Or you linger in the pool hall, later than late,
Only to scratch, pocketing the eight ball
When you had called another shot
And arrive chagrined for your date
Who says, with a smile, "Now I've
Really got you by . . ."
Years later, your wife, quite another
Woman, looks up from her crossword
To ask, "Do you know the word
Tatterdemalion?" As it happens
You do, not that you can remember
Using it; perhaps your grandfather had
And you return to reading *Ulysses*
Where you find it two pages later.
There must be a word for this.

Do folks who aren't readers
Trip that wire as often as we?
I guess neither you nor I
Is the one to ask,
Yet there must be a word,
Lest it just be *ad infinitum*

For once again this morning
After drafting this poem
And reading it to my wife
And sleeping in a little late
I joined her over coffee to hear
Her tell of Buddy Guy
Whose profile she'd been reading
In the *New Yorker*, a blues singer
Who fears that gorgeous tradition with its
Light touch on time and trouble may end
With him—and who owns a 1958 Edsel.

As_2O_5

Henry Bladon

A man in a blue velvet dinner jacket
arrived and stepped off his Harley.

He was wearing a silver skull ring
and a pair of blue jeans.

He really wanted to order a beer
but couldn't speak much English.

Out of the blue he passed the barman a handwritten note
on which was the formula for arsenic pentoxide.

The barman sighed as he stared at the indigo ink
(the writing really was quite beautiful).

Then the man said goodbye and
flagged down a passing taxi

he waved through the rear window
as he disappeared into the blue of the night.

Please Turn on the Light

Sharron Hough

I cannot see their reasoning
Though my logic is not strong
It's their judgement that is coloured
Then again, I could be wrong
A constant draining spiral
A vortex of despair
They call it blue: I call it black
But who are they to care
I'm not the feathers of a wren
A striking cobalt hue
I'm the shimmer of raven's wing
Melancholically imbued
And though I try to fly from this
To lift my wings and soar
An ocean's weight lies on my chest
Where sun can reach no more
Call it blue if you will
If you wish to keep it bright
But for a colour spectrum
There has to be some light

Iris Blue

Ruth Sabath Rosenthal

I saw such lightness of being
through the clear blue eyes
of the female husky

on the loose prancing
along sidewalk tail wagging upright
with what I fancied was pride

I saw that bushy tail
hanging down as I caught glimpses
of it weaving through

a maze of oncoming cars
& I shuddered at the thought
& prayed she'd run onto sidewalk

& moving towards her
I called out to her hoping to
distract her

then a flash of metal
& she was down
sprawled across asphalt

eyes wide open
pupils dilating —
blackness blotting out blue

Tassels and Silks

Tim Philippart

the time of tassels and silks
got the corn to lookin' up,
thinkin' I can touch the blue,
skitter with clouds,
tickle them for rain when I am thirsty.

but, like most species,
pollination got in the way,
had to quit school,
forget about the sky,
sell insurance in Cincinnati.

Royal

Audri Gaskins

azure pure we hang glide,
to journey life miles in style
across all earthly expanse.
hands welded statements.
have faith, as he smiles.

hope removes e, became hop to see
how far their e can go.
powdered blues blown away
and the genuine stay,
two can be one, in throes.

mountains surmise, rise – expound.
and he, while over peaks,
heart handsome as fate,
proves all truth of this weight,
and knows just a seed can reseat.

we linger as there in feathery air,
blood ink spilt to overcome fear.
as they fall they're recorded,
oh, what sweet bliss afforded.
love is so royal when clear.

God Might be a Potato

Al DeGenova

How many lies to disguise
the true answer
what does it matter.

I never learned to pray
not from nuns with their big sticks
and belts of beads

(at funerals for in-law aunts my lips move
to the Lord's Prayer like mumbling
'scuze me to push through a line of strangers),

nor from Jesuits with their black blazers
covered in cigarette ash and arrogance
who drowned me in pages of Camus.

In a primitive cabin built into a bluff
spiders and mice criss-cross
trails of ciphered verses across a rough wood table –

is it prayer without god.
Condemnation
accused of telling truth

facing eternal fires
for praying with pagan insects at sunset,
or the cold back of disgust

for *saying I don't really care
that much* to celebrate
the company's up year

with a rare bottle of Opus One,
there is no music at that party.
Fire me or send me to the guillotine.

I don't care, really. God might be a potato.
Eat them baked or raw
what does it matter

as long as we dance like so many Zorbas
hand in hand, when our dreams and stone walls
fall into the indigo sea.

The Last Decent Man

Corey Mesler

The firefighter and his daughter: it's
a story we've been told and still
tell. When he is named his name
is air; he is taller than moral law.
Named, he is the last decent man.
And when she is named it is sun-
shine and blue skies; she is
radiant as smiling dawn. She is the
firefighter's daughter and, today, this
is what she is called. This story is
lighter than air. It is flame; it burns
and is over. Yet, there is more,
for we continue to tell the story and
with each telling the fates change,
of the firefighter and his daughter,
but the sky is bluer, and the memory
of the story is now the story itself, amen.

Fragile Mineral Rights

Piet Nieuwland

Of moons collapsed by distance
And the solitude of an immense sky hanging
With a typhoon in hand
Its hyetograph on a heliotrope postcard
Her long dark hair splits the afternoon in two
An intense gaze drowning in the nuptial silence
Of a pair of eyes
We assemble impoverished shadows
In air humid with the weight of tears
Drink in a view of subtle exclamations
Encouraged by laden plum trees and banana,
Glimpses of rivers that joins all the sinuous
Ridged horizons of prayers and flags
Of murmurs, rushes, zephyrs
Concatenations in the warming flesh of air
Its fine bone structure of fragments
That knit the winds
Blue serum

Reflections

Doug Jacquier

For you and I,
all things seem possible when we look across blue water
from the solid shore
Peering towards the horizon,
we conspire towards a thousand buoyant courses.

Imagining a receding shore and a rising tide,
we do not weigh our stamina against the undertow
nor the wind strength against our craft;
we have enough gods
to warrant speculation.

But there are those who stand upon the solid shore
who are already at the end of this world
(and the next)
and our imagined journeys
are their fated drownings.

For them,
as they squint anxiously across the water
imagining a receding shore and a rising tide,
sailing into the blue
seems a truly godless journey.

So they sit watching us,
like hermit crabs,
waiting for us to set out,
assuming we are unlikely to return,
and picturing life inside our empty shells.

John and Mary Sing the Blues

Jan McCarthy

There were moments when they should have parted,
many, many,
but the sex was good,
familial expectations loomed,
the venue had been booked,
Here comes the bride was playing...

Blue balloons, a midnight ambulance dash,
A move from the city condo was a must
To suburban house set back with sky-blue shutters.
But curtains twitched. They hushed their arguments.

A spur-of-the-moment buy, blue-gum-ringed cottage,
A smallholding – everyone was doing it –
for irritable, asthmatic, insolent kids.
The years of toil for fruit and veg organic,
They told themselves they worked well as a team,
digging and composting,
the worm-eaten apples a missed metaphor,
no time to think or speak, or anything.

Wrinkles multiplying, blue tracery of leg-veins,
he adopted pyjamas, she read romance novels
shaking her head at lies young girls are told.
Blue funk of lonely death held them in thrall.

Last Christmas, visitors, joyless-dutiful,
Found them blackened, dry under blue quilt
she had dreaming stitched for her trousseau
(over which she'd dropped too many tears).
They buried them together, figuring
They'd choose to be united. They were wrong.

Song of Summer Night

Mir-Yashar Seyedbagheri

She loves the song of the summer atop the mountain. This is her spot, a spot she goes to night after night, always at dusk, that moment when pink and purple blend in an explosive symphony, sun setting, surrendering to the night with good cheer. There are no cities in view, hidden by the hillsides, the curves of the roads and valleys, no belligerent drivers, no boozing, depressed souls slinking down side streets and alleyways. There is only her, the night, which deepens from lavender and pink, into lush blue, into a velvet. Moon rises, a smiling luminous face, rising slowly, slowly, fully, like someone emerging from a stage. Showtime. Crickets call and the frogs join in. The sounds of voices evaporate into nothingness, people evaporate from her consciousness, replaced by night sounds. The rivers rush and whisper, breathless hush, meandering, curving along their journey. The crickets deepen their song. Tender breeze dances with the trees, arms slender and graceful in the night.

Atop the mountain, she feels bigger than the world itself, than the trivialities, the power games, the mendacities, the weariness below, hatred begetting hatred, conflict like a fungus, bills and obligations, and a world of cynics who seek negativity, who wear nastiness like a mustache. Here she can reach for the moon, for the stars that whisper and wink, silver beings aloft a velvet, lush sky. She can reach and reach, feeling the wind, the expanse, feeling so much, athwart this mountain, this silent evening. She stands astride the peaks for as long as she can, the night deepening, the moon dancing through wisp clouds, disappearing, reappearing but she is not fazed. She stays as long as she can, before the world calls her back, vows to return to this spot, night after night.

Blue mackerel

Allan J. Wills

Flesh translucent
sticky gel
perfect bait
for another
mackerel mate
Hooked
harried by 'couta
— worthless bony
big-mouthed
wormy gourmands
Ever so
a death race

First fish
filleted fresh
lime juice
spice
Ceviche
Lest
Stunned
sunned on deck
becomes a flesh squish
an opaque wreck

Shelved wracks
tinned or smoked
wrapped
for supermarket scavengers
One half off
penny pinchers
and penniless
choosers scoff
at any less
Price point
a canny epitaph
for the finny too

Out of the Blue

Charlotte McCormac

'Now you will write about last week's Ascension,'
said our teacher as we drew out our books.
On a grey morning, the whole school stood;
each of us queuing for a coloured balloon.

We flung paint splatters at the overcast horizon.
Mine was blue, ready to burst its turquoise hue.
Unseen angels' wings pulled us towards Heaven,
and colliding stars stained the whitewashed sky.

I didn't get a chance to write any more,
for someone had just arrived at the door.
The head had come to show us a picture;
my balloon had flown the furthest of all.

An old man, holding my deflated balloon
had found it unexpectedly, he hadn't a clue,
had found it unexpectedly, quite out of the
blue.

Midday Sky

Beverly M. Collins

I often carried my emotions like a folder
under my arm. A bit of feeling I could open
at will. I sometimes gazed out of my window
at the blue skies dabbed with clouds on a
soft journey. They looked down and wondered
Why I stood still when life offered much
to travel to. All the bottled blue inside to leave
behind.

Like the time I traded glances with a
quiet man seated on the bus stop bench.
The corners of his mouth pointed downward.
Oh! The blue in his heart appeared to have
flooded the color of his eyes.
Our stare was broken by the hover of a
hummingbird… A surprise that elevated
both of our expressions into a duet of
smiles.

Claustrophobia

Rosie Sandler

It's the smell of him:
pepperoni meeting liver
and fried onions in a café

where the tables sweat.
She tries to wash it off,
but it clings like musk,

marking her as his.
At night, when he lays
her down and covers

her mouth with his,
she feels the air turn
thin, her lips blue,

hands flapping
– a landed fish.
She thinks of leaving:

slipping on the shoes
she keeps ready
and walking.

She thinks, too, of worse:
of puncturing him, hearing
his own air hiss out:

a sex doll deflating.

She'd fold him neatly,
tuck him in a drawer,
then scrub the house,

floor to ceiling, until
the only smell was the
lemon-sharp scent of relief.

Big Sea

Alan Fyfe

The Windex soaking into the Jiffy Towel; chemical colour thinning out in paper valleys. It's enough to think of sitting on the rocks at Silver Sands Beach, 3 AM. That quiet hour-and-a-half between the last furtive meth deal in the carpark and the first fishers of morning. Alone with the sound of the waves, their weight, their massive violence. And that's enough to imagine calloused hands on ropes and machine hatches, as though unspoken knowledge could draw the charcoal lines between breath and Ophelia's dream, somewhere out past where day has already met with the troubled blue.

Life Imitates Art

Colleen Moyne

My childhood
was paint by numbers,
follow directions,
use only the palette provided
and never colour outside the lines

My youth
was copy and paste,
emulate the style of peers,
and trace over curves
where inspirational others had drawn before

There was a time
when all that I could see
were rain-soaked blues and greys,
running in rivulets down empty pages
obscuring the bigger picture.

But now my life
is free-form and flowing,
all the colours of autumn
laid out before me
and still time to create a masterpiece.

Dawn

Karen Louise

Birds sing.
Black night turns to blue-grey
while the sun hides behind the horizon.
I sit on the edge of the bed,
winter socks on the bedroom floor.

That moment when sleep pulls me more
than staying awake – I sit with that.
On the edge of the bed,
winter socks on the bedroom floor.

Feel the fog inside my head clear,
Roll my shoulders and stretch my arms.
as wide as that fish I know my grandpa never caught.
Give thanks that my body allowed me
one more breath,
one more hour,
one more day.
As I sit on the edge of the bed,
winter socks on the bedroom floor.

Betta Fish

Jay McPherson

The somnambulist dances, its twist
and pull muted in motion.
In the corner, a faux skull sleeps,
maw open, teeth bared, the bed
waits, a quilt of bubbles
begging it to breathe.
Gray tugs at its edges, rot creeping in
to the liquid flamenco of cobalt
seas that fade into crimson ink.
Yet the dance continues, untethered, unfazed,
anchored in the reality of a dream.
Content to one world inside another,
nothing ends at the beginning
and things start new.
Forgetting the tears of yestermorrow,
I warm in the arms of a clear nothing,
I cool beneath the glass of something else,
a room within a room houses blue.

Half-Life

Winston Plowes

For those who served at the British Nuclear Test Site
Maralinga, South Australia 1956-63

there were men who scrabbled together
their untethered thoughts
still swimming in the soup of war –
solitary and screwed down
by the light and heat

and there were tiny spaces
lost in each of their heads
like patches of sky
where a slate used to be

and now there's a new home
for those glimmers of blue
where they stored their worlds
now that some have decided to listen
to songs that have reached a half-life of sorts

The Blue Fields

Patricia Unsworth

Bright as a summer sky sprinkled with clouds
Waves of blue, blurred lightly with white and red,
Bow into a gentle breeze that shimmers
As a vast Mediterranean Sea.

In haste the growing stalks of flax reach up
'Til petals drop and fields of blue turn brown.
Bearded seeds rattle in late summer winds
As harvest draws the season to its close.

With beauty gone, the flax succumbs to fate
As toiling reapers tread through endless fields
To pull with hardened hands the precious stalks
Whose silky fibres feed the mills.

The strands of flax spun to the finest yarn
Fill endless looms, which clatter back and forth,
Never-ending, through day and night, and where,
Heads bowed to task, the mill girls' lives are spent.

Whilst one year's yield is turned to linen cloth
Again fields are harrowed, the seed is sown,
The soil as bleak as life within the mills
Until, once more, the sunlit fields are blue.

Blue Kisses

Alyson Faye

Dewy youngsters tig-tagging
through fields. Picking blackberries
you gave me my first kiss
with juice stained lips
leaving a mulberry bruise
in the shape of your mouth.

Skirt billowing at Blackpool
in the shadow of the Pleasure Beach,
camera bedecked, you blew me
a pungent salt and chip kiss,
with lips chilled blue by winter's chafe.

A seagull swooping,
stole that floating kiss
carrying it skywards.

Later, your blue kisses
took me to new places.
Long, lazy weekends snatched
from our families' gaze.

Strumming your guitar
at a blowsy gig,
you riff the last few bars,
bend down to whisper
from behind the mic —

"To the lady who taught me
 how to beat the blues."

Blue Evening

Wilda Morris

Blueberry buckle, muffins,
pancakes, pie al la mode,
or those soft blue marbles,
sweet and shiny,
tossed into a fruit salad. . . .

Best of all, though, is to sit
on a bench in the garden
surrounded by delphinium
and forget-me-nots
as indigo buntings flit
around egg-filled nests
in nearby shrubs
and cobalt sky darkens

fingers bluing as I reach into
an azure-rimmed bowl,
plop the juicy little globes into your mouth
one
       by
              one
and you pop them into mine.

Scarcity Blessing

Ann Neuser Lederer

Across the last blue sky
of Indian Summer, a quote
unfurled in the slanted rays:
"In the midst of abundance,"
    it proclaimed,
"Appreciation falters."

Although I may not name
the author, its theme
reverberated,
reframing, like a therapist.
I dared not attempt its reversal,
exposing the lining hidden
in the cloud:

"Scarcity fosters fondness,"
whispered the new banner,
waving its words above
the crusted seed pods
of once profligate Morning Glories.

The long shadows of the newly bared
trees' arms reached and entwined,
despite air now chilled with promises –
or memories – of warmth.

The Novice

Cynthia Leslie-Bole

I yearn to be
a simpleton
a devotee of
sweet
slow
Simplicity

I weave
garlands
of indigo gentian
to decorate
her hair

I sweep
golden pollen
over her
contented lids

I trickle
crystal water
into her
receptive lips

I sit calmly
at her feet
matching
my breath
to hers

I aspire
to become
Simplicity's
high priestess
performing rites
appropriately sparse
to honor her

I pray
for her chants
to wash me
clean
like a flash flood
scouring
the canyonlands
of convoluted constructs

no matter how often
I fail and flail
into complexity
and chaos
I humbly resume
my practice
without defense

because
only the balm
of quiet truth
can grace
Simplicity's altar

when I renew
my vows
she welcomes
me back
into her
spare temple
decorated
only
with light
Who does not want to be the one amongst all

The Notebook

Ilona Hegedus

I was looking at the view from the window
of a café downtown, though I was trying to concentrate
on the writing.
When the tram stopped outside, and people got off,
I was thinking about buying a pizza on the way home.
So much for concentration...

On the way to success, there are lots of failures
and lots of lessons learnt.
Bad decisions are like bad poems, though
only from the right distance.

Here's a notebook with indigo cover. It's a present
from my friends.
I must write another poem now,
because it is there to be used.

Green on blue

Mantz Yorke

'Green on blue', they call it,
when Afghan police (or maybe
militants dressed as police)
shoot British troops. Nothing new:

yet another loved one
opens the front door,
sees a soldier on the step,
knows the worst.

Now the ritual homecoming:
the stubby grey C-17A
sinks from the blue sky
to the still, green, sunlit land,

touches down, comes to a stop,
lowers its ramp. Smartly,
soldiers bear a flag-draped
coffin to each attending hearse.

Later, young and old
stand in silence at the roadside,
unshowily, their heads bowed,
as the cortege passes by.

Green on blue – the glory
of an English summer day
once more turned upside down
by the converging lens of grief.

Childhood Toys

Carl 'Papa' Palmer

After two hours reuniting with
twenty year old toys stored
in the attic since he was ten,
Star Wars, He-Man and
Transformers, he demonstrates,
with authentic sound effects,
how the blue car can be changed
into a robotic mechanical man.

His wife only sees how her husband
transforms into a ten-year-old boy.

The Less Busy Season

Josh Lefkowitz

I have been a flower shop in February
or a pie emporium near the end of November
Busy! I guess, is another way to say it
every idea or image clamoring for attention –
"Take a number," I'd shout from behind the counter,
"yes, please, I'll get to you, promise!"

But now I am in an extended prolonged quiet
like an indigo-obsessed Spaniard, 1901-1904
only instead of blue there's...nothing
"Papa," my imaginary children worry,
"are we going to have to close the store?"
(When I say 'imaginary children' I mean future poems)

Nonsense, I reply, kissing the tops of their heads,
someone will always need a rose/pie/this,
and indeed it comes – one friend gets married,
another's mother dies, a leaf leaps from its branch,
or I manage to forget everything I've done before today
and I'm back in business, baby!

Mediocrity

Samuel Gulliksson

I wondered how many
we are who love blue
potatoes, just because
they are blue
(even though they're not).

I thought the few of us
could change the world
but then I learned
blue is everyone's favourite colour.

In my house, a conspiracy

Mera Baid Kaur

In my house, a conspiracy brewing
in an already burnt and tinged pan
the children do the cooking
their backs turn, shooting glances that stop
at my door... lit by dampened light
just whispered past curtains
the path of my chaos littered
long before my profile manifests
from the darkened corner. I'm already entombed
waiting for masculine hands to take
my words, strangle them, bleed them free of air
wrinkle them 'til they can't straighten out again
stunned blinkless: the ultra-violet iris sprays
bringing colour and screaming beauty
to the wood-grain overcasting my vision
'til it bursts with the faded cyan of melting glaciers
I hurry, tighten my face, catch the warming waters
with this buoyant body– eyes reflecting its sinking end.

blue beaches

Bernise Carolino

some wait for storms,
that thunderclap of limbs
lost to currents unknown,

but I say wade in by choice,
bleach your bones
driftwood white,

crown your hair with kelp,
reshape your fingers
after starfish,

swallow saltwater
and welcome the blur
over your vision,

unlearn your love
for the hot glitter of sand,
for even when the blue

beaches you like a whale,
ensnaring the next sailor
with its sirens,

you'll find silver scales
and strains of song
under your skin, in your lungs.

Ye Olde Gaol Cell

Ruth Z. Deming

The asylum doors
Are cold and gray
Inside a bitter fate
Awaits those not
Helped yet by the great
Doctor Benjamin Rush.
One man sitting on a bale of hay
In the dank basement sips on
Watered-down milk
They will whip him again today
To rid him of his frenzy
All he sees before him are colors
Gorgeous colors
They're back again, he shouts
Pink, rose, purple, blue, indigo
Spectacular indigo, covering
The walls, the ceilings, the bars
Cold and gray.
When the gaolers return
They rub their eyes and speak
In low tones.
The man may be an idiot, they say,
But, bye our leave, the man's
Become a saint.

I wish you were awake, Luther

Claudia Bierschenk

You sleep through the storm.

While your father watches from the top floor
window, I pace the hall

and imagine you between us,
one chubby hand on the glass,

hear that musical Oh... from your lips,
as you take in this new wonder in your life.

Lightning reflects in your eyes,
whose colour has slowly started

changing from blue to grey
or green.

I count the seconds between
flash and thunder,

I wish you were awake, so you could see.

Where I Walk in Denali

Lucy Tyrrell

I. beneath the blue

third week in May
either side of road
snow lingers
not in tatters
but as soft, layered quilt

white broken by
gray-green spruce spires
ridge rocks
dark lace of dwarf birch branches

wind whisks away
white-crowned sparrow's song
landscape overdue for melt
until white is green
beneath the blue

II. eclipse by raven

a change of brightness—
barely perceptible

shadow skims the road
spilled-ink feathers
sheer the blue—
raven heading east
silent wings glissade

when low-flying raven
masks sunlight—
a delight for longer
than its fleeting
traverse of wings

The Alice-Blue Nightie of Sweet Aphrodite

Ken Gosse

One low of birth but great of girth
loved Aphrodite's naughty nightie.
Was this any cause for fuss?
I'll tell you ('tween the two of us,
although I never spread a rumor,
this one puts me in the humor)
for her bloomers' disappearance
had to do with non-adherence
of two roomers at the inn,
a comic team—one fat, one thin—
when she was ready to begin
her show of skills which always thrills
the audience (which pays her bills),
but these two chaps—by chance, perhaps—
had let their weekly payment lapse
(for once again their fortune flew
on wings of dice beyond the blue);
they had no money for her honey,
nor the nectar for the lector
who would read some nonsense verse
while they mimed long what should be terse.

These very two pantomimists
whose act, next up on stage, consists
of making fun by making faces,
hoping that good humor's graces
graced their purses, stopped reverses of their fortune,
not requiring some importune
actions to be made on stage
which often caused the crowds to rage
and meant, sometimes, they must abandon
obscure towns before they land in
gaoler's care for one more night,
without the fare to have the right
of room and board before the horde
(which follows them, with hand on sword)
delivers them unto their lord—
the sheriff, who must pay a tariff
to his liege should they aggrege
the toll for every road that's traveled
by each minion, else they're gaveled
and they'll spend the night in jail
'lest their wives, who are true-blue,
will "post their bail" a time or two.

So, what became of gown so naughty,
worn by beauty, flaunting, bawdy,
and her retinue (those ladies
whom most wives say come from Hades—
lovely maids of many shades,
from cream to darkest marmalades,
who dance with polka-dots of red
tied to a G-string by a thread,
and sometimes blue, their small tutu
the sheerest for the clearest view)?

Praetorians-R-Us were hired
(they're the ones she most admired)
as her guard while she's enchanting
diverse mobs, their raves and ranting
sometimes losing all control,
although that was, in part, her goal,
but when the mimes began Act Two
ahead of when their turn was due,
the crowd, a wild and raving child,
advanced and yelled and nearly felled
the theater and dressing rooms
so all the ladies and their grooms
made haste to taste the wine then fled
through every door, from every bed:
half dressed—their costumes so impressed
the town's men, they snatched off the street
each lass 'fore stones might hurt her feet.

Both hesitant and very flighty,
Aphrodite lost her nightie.
Fearing to entrust the yokels
she sought help from backup vocals
(one she can't afford to lose,
her countertenor played the blues),
the same, who'd never let her down
ensured they'd both get out of town
and though her nightie stayed behind
she borrowed his—he didn't mind—
the burly and androgynous
Homogenous Erogenous.

Color of Paint

Jan Chronister

I paint my bedroom
with a color called Nostalgia,
a neutral beige
I've seen before
in nursing homes, doctors' walls
and gray-haired ladies' blouses.

Paint over a blue
the hue of cornflowers,
delphiniums, afternoon sky,
blue I've matched
my dreams with for twenty years
and now I'm tired of it.

I want to sleep with a color
that leaves me alone.

Walking Out, Walking In

Mark A. Murphy

Not one footpath, but many paths
as we pass white flowering blackthorn

shouldering holly, hawthorn and elder,
past the age-old dance of wild borage

and blue and white honesty propagating
along the roadside. Through field and stile

into caerulean woodland beyond design.
Far beyond the serpent's head of beech

and broken backs of last year's bracken.
Where the ballet of this year's bluebells

plays itself out under a canopy of oak,
birch, and the enchantment of bird song.

Doesn't anybody make blue movies anymore?

Allen Ashley

No, I don't mean the titillation
and fleshpot flicks of old seedy
Soho but rather a realistic
depiction of how hard and unsatisfying
life mostly is. You dream
of making it; you never do. You
dream of escaping the place
you were born; you never will.
We used to call this stuff gritty
urban realism or kitchen
sink. Nowadays it's been soaped
out into unconvincing melodrama.

But would I even watch those downbeat
films? I'm more likely to listen
to my blues. Bessie, Billie, BB
and all the Delta boys. Moving on
through Clapton, Page and Plant,
Jim, Janis and Jimi. On Neil Young's album
"On The Beach" he has "Revolution
Blues", "Vampire Blues" and "Ambulance
Blues". In that order. Sounds
about right.

off-colour

Jill Vance

blue like the med in the summer sun
blue like the sky with contrails
blue like the eyes that you want to melt in

if only it could be that way
but it's so different

instead it's …

blue like dying stars no longer to twinkle
blue like unseen trickling tears
blue like emptiness devoid of description

but it could be so different
if only i could find a way

instead it's …

how it is
so much more than being off-colour
and far beyond being blue

Blue Period

Linda Barrett

PMS is in me
I can't stop crying
Over the slightest things
Write in my robin's egg notebook
All the insults real and imagined
With peacock colored ink
Tears spatter onto the pages
As I squeeze a navy blue pimple
A cyst full of liquid and dead blood
This is what I face
Every month before my period comes
To liberate me from my depression.
.

Blue

April Miller

Blue
River, Sea, Sky and Calm.
Swish, Ripple, Swoosh and Tranquil.
Relaxed, Holiday, Centred and Actualised.
Life as it should be.

Red
Fire, Winter Leaves, and Anger Streams.
Crackle, Crunch, Prickle and Harm.
Jostled, Watchful, Alert and Unsettled.
Life as it is.

More blue for the human to float in the dream.
Grandson paints a picture,
What is it Grandma needed to ask?
Why blue of course, What more do you want?

Layers of Blue

Kathryn Sadakierski

Fish scales, turquoise in pearlescent swirls
Against the teal of the ocean waves,
Blue alongside blue,
Leading back to you
And those original feelings
Pointing back

To blue,
More than the hue of skies, azure
Above aquamarine flowers
And Delft pottery, Prussian blue
Motifs of windmills and farmhouses
Seeing life through cerulean lenses.

The rush for tulips,
Blooms for everyone to cherish
Before spring faded with the scrapbook pages
Yellowed by the light of winter's half-closed eyes,
Nothing like the gravity that pulled us to
Planets and stars aligned in the heart,
Indigo blue,
The color swept into ocean tranquility,
Horizon lines comforting the mind.

Blue, a many-paletted thing,
The hue you can't shake
As it paints your heart,
Every surface
Ringing truer than the melodies of a harp.

Gramercy, All Hallows Eve

Terry White

      It came time to check the wine,
blintzes, pelmeni, hors d'oeuvres.
She left loverboy there,
in the dark of the bay window.
Beyond the marsh hawk's nest, children dance
around pyres of cane. Flame and smoke
from petrochemical plants
boil above St. James Parish.
      They hear her step from kitchen: cook's women,
all gabbling with their hands. She replies
in Cajun, German, Spanish.
Light winks from goblet and cutlery.
Cook pins a monkfish to the table. It wriggles
as the cleaver slices through backbone.
Cook's fingers sluice bloody ribbons:
egg sac, heart, liver fall out. Cook squeezes out more filth.
      The air turns rancid like menses. Someone speaks.
A plate falls. Ortolans crackle in grease.
Soon guests will don their hoods to catch spatter.
That sound of spiny feet or bills clattering onto china.
Knows the rosettes of blood dotting white linen.
She feels a knocking in her chest;
ashes form in her mouth. This old sadness
like a guest she cannot send away—
Exsanguinated, a vampire of no desire.

      He turns from the window to catch her eye.
A murmur:
Those godawful children from the fields,
The pyramids of burning cane—
Come dancing, come dancing,
blue faces into the hall.

Gift

Mary Anna Kruch

What is your Gift to the Universe?
The memory of first light upon your lover's cheek
    moments before awakening?
The music of sparrows at dawn?
The joy of an indigo sky at dusk?
    At this moment, our tour bus threads
    seamlessly through coastal roads carved
    into the Lattari Mountains
    toward the Amalfi Coast.
    The farthest hills appear and reappear
    in shades of gray to sea green,
    tempered by thick clouds;
    air is transmuted to silver.
    From deep, ancient rock crevices
    laurel grows in spice-scented sprays –
    like flushed cheeks upon wizened faces
    that watch us along our narrow track.
    We journey west into Campagna,
    peer through windows –
    elated by the noon sun's luster
    on a turquoise Tyrrhenian Sea.
    At this moment, we feel the cool breeze
    taking in the ocean air
    that smiles with familiarity –
    recognizing   the rhythm   of an ancestor's heart.

The universe does not promise forever.
Release your passion
your poetry –
return   these   moments   to the universe,
give heart   where hearts are broken.
This is your gift.

Blue Sky Piggy Blimp Kamikaze

Gerard Sarnat

Six helicopters circle the blue.
Un/marked cop or military
state vehicles well as huge

detours keep us away
from our nearby home
plus The People's POTUS.

One ominous man in dark
glasses warns me that political
poetry may be criminal.

Here in elite Silicon Valley's
concrete California (where
Hillary won big) dreamin'

reality show, troops mass
at Portola Valley's border
(Westridge's Ford Field)

in advance of touted
visit this afternoon
to cart off money bags

which high-tech titans
and libertarians now hope
will keep Trump as Prez.

We stop by a hardware store
to buy lotta manure fertilizer,
some chemicals, two remotes

then consult McVeigh's how-to script
before loading booty into cement
mixer on his motorcade route.

To make carbon of diamonds

Gretel Bull

Neptune's lapis orb
turns calmly –
a tempting jewel to reach for perhaps,
when our homes have finished
burning.

Is there gravity on Mars?
Sin?
Perhaps redemption?
How many trillion light years must man travel
to forgive himself?

What of Saturn – gussied in her
looted jewels?
A great canary diamond glut
with precious water,
surely?

The dwarf, Pluto
counts itself lucky,
too small to sustain the life of
cannibals
like us.

On earth, there is no
air.
No water.
El Niño weeps dryly,
and a sigh of red dust shrouds the sky.

Fires sear our verges,
no rains quell the desert heart –
where gussets of air lay densely,
thick as lies.

Out in the desperate blue of the Pacific,
our neighbours
shall soon be on the ocean floor,
everything azure.

The sea,
so many thousand years away,
writhes, in the colours of Cezanne –

rabid violets of skies
that become mountains that become roof tops –
hiding bruises and brides,
chaos, dreams and
nothingness.

We are passengers,
on this great hurtling eyeball of water and light.
Birds of war have snuffed out
so many
lovely things.

I have no crest to fall,
no tiny bubble of screaming
nascent awareness,
warning me to
stand down.

The ego, raves and crows,
receding,
not nearly long enough for us to
understand a thing –

perhaps,
in the blue before sleep,
or in sleep itself,
or the eternal cobalt of death.

Nursing home visit, with cornflowers

Lynn Woollacott

Cornflowers, droop in a grey vase,
mother slumps in a winged green chair –
dribbles. Her one working arm
snakes the blurry air.

Cornflowers, blue, like sky, and the painted room
alive with blackfly. Mother says she's been invaded
through the open window, but she knows,
gives me the evil eye.

Cornflowers, dropped in a beige bin.
I call for someone to hunch mother back up
to some semblance of sitting,
she slips down further in the chair.

Cornflowers, crushed. Mother mumbles
a girl played draughts with her, made her laugh.
Now mother weeps and keeps weeping. I hold
on to the open door willing someone to come.
just to be alone again.

An Angel in a Blue Prius

Joanne Jagoda

I didn't know I'd encounter an Angel who drives a blue Prius
on one of my twenty-five trips to the city.
Getting off at Montgomery St. Bart station by 7:30,
I watch the city wake up like a sleepy toddler.
Spiffy, decked out in a cool scarf,
eyebrows filled in, new red shoes,
joining the stream of the dot-commers
charging up the escalator;
absorbed, clutching cell phones, rushing to Starbucks,
I act regular, like I'm going to work like they are,
but I break away from the herd to get to my appointment.
I hop on the 38 Limited, sit with the locals armed with their
bus passes, and shopping bags.
Harried fathers tote babies to daycare;
a scary, leather-clad woman curses to no one in particular.
I gaze out at the urban blight— scrawled graffiti tags,
homeless sprawled in doorways,
sleeping in on their cardboard featherbeds.
The bus passes through Japantown; I get off at Divisadero,
walk two blocks, spritz my hands
with foam cleanser in the lobby,
go down to the basement, check in,
change into the crappy gown that never closes right.
I smile and greet the regulars in the waiting room.
I'm called in. My techs joke while they position me precisely.

The machine-monster whirrs and skims over me
for twelve minutes,
while Frank Sinatra croons in the background.
I contemplate, pray, but I refuse to feel sorry for myself.
I'm done, get dressed, go out, but the 9:05 bus is late,
so I call UBER.
I realized later it was the way it was supposed to be.
The handsome, foreign driver in a blue Prius was chatty,
talking about last night's Giants game,
I'm quiet at first. He knew I came from the hospital,
checked me out in the rear view.
I adjust my burgundy scarf. I'm still vain; I'm still me.
"How're you doing?" he pipes up like he really wants to know.
"I'm making it," I tell him. "Radiation, you know,
is way easier than chemo."
Then we chit chat and discover we both have three daughters.
Bonded now like fast friends, he heads down Post St.,
grins at me through the rear view.
"You still have work to do you know," he declares
when we're almost at Bart.
I smile thinking he is surely a messenger-angel.
"I'll be ready when the time comes," I answer with confidence.
"Have a good day," I say, as he drops me at the station.
"And thanks."
"Have a good life," he calls out to me. "And be well."

A Bunch of Things god Doesn't Deserve

Michael T. Coolen

respect
so forget the capital letters
god doesn't get them
he/she/it isn't a city or a country
July can be capitalized
but not jahweh
Amsterdam deserves a capital A
but not allah

ice cream
iced lattes
ice fishing
a good Chianti
let him make his own wine
Peshawarian tandoori chicken
Rainier green death beer
strawberry-rhubarb pie
Laphroiag, capital L, single malt
fish and chips
day-old pizza
Rolaids

a vacation on the Big Island
on any island
peninsula
tropical coastline
surfing paddle boarding
bungee-jumping
skin diving
luaus
downhill skiing
sunsets
Broadway musicals

a great orgasm with some you love
any kind of family life
children
look how he treated Jesus
a warm hot tub
after skinny-dipping in the ocean
with your squeeze-du-jour
tic tacs when a mermaid surfaces
out of nowhere in the hot tub
and asks for a threesome
dancing with a daughter at her wedding
sitting with you in the pews at the funeral
for your son returned from war
any funeral or memorial for any child
who died before his four score and a few

Christmas
Saturnalia belongs to the Romans
Solstice
Diwali
let him find his own holiday
let him have April 1st
Easter
just stop with the crucifixion on Good Friday

unconditional understanding
unconditional forgiveness
the unconditional love of a dog
who can play dead better than god
unconditional anything 'cuz…
just 'cuz

finally
listening to the blues
Delta
Detroit
country
cross-over
any of the Kings
B.B.
Albert
Freddie
Big Mama Anybody
Big Daddy Anybody
Anybody whose name begins with B

Bessie
Bobby
Big Bill
Blind Lemon
'cuz' god caused most of misery for everybody
during their already too short time on Earth
which is their home and deserves a capital E
by god

Variations in the Perception of Color

Howard Brown

One's perception of color depends on the precise wavelength of light—calibrated in nanometers—to which the eye is exposed.

Of course, exactly what a nanometer may be is yet another question and one which, in my eighth decade, I no longer care to master.

But I do know that once seen, a color can be conjured by the mind without the benefit of any light whatsoever.

And in this alternative, nether world, it's emotion, not nanometers, by which things are measured.

Thus, when I lie in bed at 3:00 a.m. and reflect on some of the more grievous errors I've made in life, it's blue I see.

Not as something the eye registers, but a
phenomena which floods my neural pathways,
a synesthetic connection, if you will.

It's not the bright, crystalline blue of the
daytime sky, nor the somewhat softer blue
you associate with a newborn baby boy.

No, this is a darker blue, more closely akin
to an overripe plum, reflecting detachment,
dejection and a profound sense of sadness.

So, remember friend, the color the eye
beholds is not necessarily the one which may
fill the heart.

Airport Interlude

Marsha Mittman

Sitting in an airport restaurant
Angry at an extended layover
Canned songs blasting
The food vile, the prices high
Can't even log on to my computer

Suddenly, unexpectedly, there's music
Real music – a live guitar –
In an airport restaurant there's
Actually a real guy, singing live
Chatter shifts to hush, to listen

The vibe changes – instantly –
Our plastic, packaged, rushed world
Smiles and relaxes while listening
To harmonies flying up into the
Blue alongside the departing planes

Sky is the Dream of Trees

Brad Rose

The most trusted people in America are actors.
I have the receipts.

Consider the invention of daylight savings time.
What on earth could make the sun set so late?

You need not bother finishing your sentences.
Say what you will, they speak for themselves.

Just as a roof is indifferent to the logic of rain,
sleep is uninterested in the meaning of dreams.

Due to the blind justice of sin,
anyone can find the devil.

Flies won't land on Zebras.
Flies don't like stripes.

Because I have a lot in common with myself,
I'm interested only in the outside of things.

Beneath the still, blue, sleep of the sky, the trees rock impatiently.
Is there somewhere more important they ought to be?

On the island again

John Bost

I got up early on the island.
I didn't want to miss a moment.
Coffee in hand, off to the deck I went.
The water held my gaze, as boats passed by.

I didn't want to miss a moment.
We skipped rocks, and looked for sea glass.
The water held my gaze, as boats passed by.
A sunny ferry ride to Winter Harbor was wonderful.

We skipped rocks and looked for sea glass.
Was that a fossilized whoopie pie I found?
A sunny ferry ride to Winter Harbor was wonderful.
Then all of us biked out to Schoodic Point.

Was that a fossilized whoopie pie I found?
I uncovered treasured rocks and broken shells, beachcombing.
Then all of us biked out to Schoodic Point.
I can't forget our lobster dinner at Abel's.

I uncovered treasured rocks and broken shells, beachcombing.
Sitting on Sand Beach, I had breakfast of o.j.
      and the Atlantic Ocean.
I can't forget our lobster dinner at Abel's.
We sat outside around a picnic table, as the sun set.

Sitting on Sand Beach, I had breakfast of o.j.
      and the Atlantic Ocean.
Climbing the rocks, I paused and saw moments from years ago.
We sat outside around a picnic table, as the sun set.
There was ice cream for dessert in Bar Harbor.

Climbing the rocks, I paused and saw moments from years ago.
We'd unfurl the towels and put on some Sea and Ski.
There was ice cream for dessert in Bar Harbor.
Marshmallows were roasted and sangria savored.

I got up early on the island.

How Can You Say That?

William Butler

She repeats that to me,
I mull it over,
I say, "It's easy, watch"
and I slowly enunciate those words,
each formed precisely, plainly on my lips,
and she actually watches closely, avidly.
It's then I feel a sudden flush engulf my face,
probably foul my heart, too,
with the cobalt coldness of shame.
"How can you say that?"
I shouldn't have said it, no, I should not.
And now I can find no way to turn back,
find the roundabout
leading me away from this wrong way home.

Fringe Dwellers' Sonnet

Matthew Horsfall

Nine a.m. Already there is no shade.
Dawn frost turns to daylight and scorches the earth.
Drought drains the wetlands as they sink and fade
into wastelands. A sense of self worth
shrinking ever deep. The growing divide
between the newly minted suburbs sprawling
and blood bone dusty dying streets. Our high tide
rises relentless. Old storm clouds are calling
to the sad sapphire eyes trapped within.
Skies ever clear. A merciless blue flame
charring the sun scarred kids with sun scarred skin.
And should the wasps colonise yet again,
long may the strength of these people resist
vaccines, teachers, fate, doctors and dentists.

Back in the Blue

Mike Hall

His eyes are blue;
misty as the hills from whence he came.
A gentle man, he sits and muses,
silent with his thoughts.
Once more he views an iridescent sea
that sparkles in the sun,
and blue-green pines
that sweep majestic to a rocky shore,
while glowing bright, a wondrous sight,
the mighty snow-capped purple mountains
forever upwards soar.
Above it all a pale blue sky
where once, with crewmates
Jack and Bill, and Pete and Will,
he often went to fly.
Old friends and dearest comrades then
but now, all sadly gone.
Yet in the twilight of his mind
their memory lingers on.
Young men who laughed and joked and swore,
who smoked and drank and called for more
and played those games that only young men can.
Lost for a cause that few could ever understand.

A gentle touch returns him
to the land of here and now.
The forests fade, the mountains and the sea recede
and in their place a cheery smile
and a welcome cup of tea.
Been somewhere nice?
He smiles and nods.
Yes thanks, I have.
I've been back up there with the bods.*

*RAF slang for squadron personnel

A Study in Indigo

Remngton Murphy

Just before the first
Silver slivers of daybreak,

Standing in a forest,
The branches draped

With luminescent blue and green
Angel-hair filaments,

Dreaming about you
I soared into a deep blue heaven.

Unable to speak, or wiggle my fingers,
My heart beating wildly,

I felt the blade of the new moon
Brush against my shoulder, leaving a tear.

The next thing I remember,
I saw your ghostly glowing face

Looming above me, your glimmering
Telepathic eyes, blue topaz,

Giving me the stare,
Whispering to me, flattering,

"You are exciting, you are special to me,
You are mine and mine only,"

As I lingered there, flat on my back
On a cold metal table,

Feeling no pain.
But now I feel it,

Now that you're gone,
And I'm pretty damn sure

Never to lift me off my feet again.
Welcome to the bright sky blue

Forever morning end of the vision,
The dreamless sleep I call this life.

Bluesville

Ryn Holmes

Blue—hearted,
Baby stands solo
on the station platform
catching a ride on the last-chance
train out of Bluesville.

Her man booked his trip
and left old baggage behind.
His comings and goings,
to-ings and fro-ings,
worth a punch to his ticket.

Smoke and ash tangle her bones,
kick her smack-dab into a train wreck
with their roles changed:
the social one now solitary,
all vices, versed.

So Baby stares down the line
as the future rumbles in,
gathers her things and climbs the steps,
sitting down in the grumbling blue beast
as it lumbers off, carries her away
far from Bluesville.

It's a hard word

Samara Shaw

I *c*an't say it,
    but
        it slung from her mouth, quick and calm like spring,
                birthing de*a*th instead of life.
It twirled a storm in our chests;
ears cracked,
noses dripped,
eyes slouched,
brows furrowed.
        Minds fell from mou*n*tains.
        Knives chopped through teeth and tongues.
A cup of blues spilled on the floor, stained the carpet, splattered
family portraits in the hall.
    It's been a rainy year,
        but the puddles are i*c*ed; no fun to jump in.
Our lives were traded
    for the headline no one expected a father to wear,
        the commercial no one paid attention to,
        the sickness no one worried about,
                and pain,
bon*e* bruising   pain.
But we trek on;
    lungs deep with air,
heavy as water.
        It is not ou*r* hallelujah.

Blueberries versus Sausages

Mark Hudson

     Today I had a physical. My physician has
been on my case to lose weight for years. I'm
almost pushing three hundred pounds.

     But today the nurse weighed me, and
I had lost a magical six pounds!

     It must be summer, and I'm getting out
and walking more. I'm not sure what I did,
but I'm inspired to keep at it!

     But then he said that recent tests showed
that I have signs of diabetes. And because of
my big belly, they have detected signs of
arthritis in the spine.

     At forty-six, I've outlived a lot of people
I've grown up with. Still, I need to at least try
to be healthy!

One thing my doctor said I need to eliminate from my diet is salt and sugar. So back home I had a bag of blueberries. I determined to go home and munch on those for dinner. But when I got home and opened the bag, there were some sausages in the bag with the blueberries, and I didn't know!

I cooked the sausages, ate them, and then took the most peaceful nap. Dreaming of the diet I would start tomorrow or sometime soon!

Forbidden Shower

Chuka Susan Chesney

Below my shower pan, there's an art opening.
I'm a fiberglass shower in a landmark building
on Glendale Boulevard next to Rockaway Records.

The curator smiles wide at art collectors
with wallets of plastic who might possibly buy
a painting or two, or maybe a sculpture.

I'm a shower in a restroom at the top of the stairs.
Guests and artists use the toilet one by one.

First in line, a lady has to pee,
next a man bolts in for fifteen minutes,
another guy comes in, combs his moustache and smooths
his beard while glancing fondly in the bathroom mirror.

A third man wanders in who appears to be homeless.

He takes off his T-shirt, his blue jeans, his shoes,
turns on the faucets, draws my vinyl curtain closed.

Downstairs everyone can hear the rush
of cascading water spattering the ceiling.
They tell the curator who becomes hopping mad.

She says, Who would take a SHOWER during
an art SHOW? And climbs the stairs, pounds on
the lavatory door. I can hear her even though

my stream's spraying out my nozzle.
Then the homeless man answers, and says, It's me.
I had to use the bathroom and I saw the shower,

I couldn't resist the luxury of pure, hot water so I stepped
inside, rinsed, and used the soap dispenser. The curator replies,
GET OUT, OR I'LL CALL THE POLICE!

She adds, If you'd only told me ahead of time
I would have helped you, but you took a shower
without asking anybody, we're having a reception!

It's time to get out now, do you have a towel?
The homeless man emerged from me and got dressed wet—
He left by the side door with no regrets.

Break Open Your Eyes

Linda M. Crate

break open the blue in your eyes
prove to me there are no demons inside

I've met too many monsters
disguised as angels

with their blue eyes
i find i don't trust them,

but dark eyes with all their mysteries
to hide seem more worthy of my trust;

i find that i trust blue eyed people less
must confess part of the problem

is all my childhood bullies had blue eyes
were praised and angels and told they were perfect—

i want you to prove to me that you are different
so i can deduce that there is someone

with eyes different than mine
that won't try to rip me apart.

About Truth Serum Press

Established in 2014, Truth Serum Press is based in Adelaide, Australia, but publishes books from authors in all parts of the English-speaking world.

Truth Serum Press (along with sister presses Pure Slush Books and Everytime Press) is part of the Bequem Publishing collective.

Truth Serum Press publishes novels, novellas, and short story collections. We no longer publish single author poetry anthologies (though sometimes when the mood strikes us, we do).

Similarly when the mood strikes us, we publish multi-author anthologies. Generally, we publish fiction … and sometimes (just sometimes) we publish non-fiction.

We publish in English, and we would gladly publish in other languages if we understood them.

We like books that take us to new places, to new experiences and inside new minds and hearts.

We also like to laugh.

If you think we might like your novel or novella or short story collection, please email truthserumpress@live.com.au.

You can also visit our website at https://truthserumpress.net/.

Also from TRUTH SERUM PRESS

truthserumpress.net/catalogue

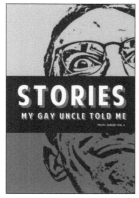  

- *Stories My Gay Uncle Told Me* Truth Serum Vol. 3
  978-1-925536-86-7 (paperback) 978-1-925536-87-4 (eBook)
- *Wiser* Truth Serum Vol. 2
  978-1-925101-31-7 (paperback) 978-1-925101-32-4 (eBook)
- *True* Truth Serum Vol. 1
  978-1-925101-29-4 (paperback) 978-1-925101-30-0 (eBook)

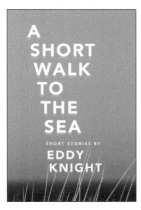 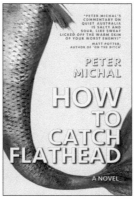 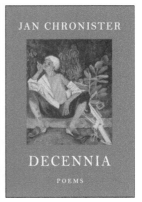

- *A Short Walk to the Sea* by Eddy Knight
  978-1-925536-01-1 (paperback) 978-1-925536-02-7 (eBook)
- *How to Catch Flathead* by Peter Michal
  978-1-925536-94-2 (paperback) 978-1-925536-95-9 (eBook)
- *Decennia* by Jan Chronister
  978-1-925536-98-0 (paperback) 978-1-925536-99-7 (eBook)

Also from TRUTH SERUM PRESS

truthserumpress.net/catalogue

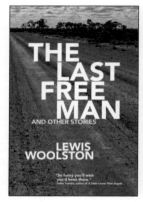  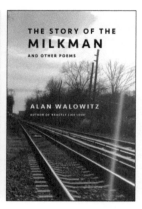

- *The Last Free Man* by Lewis Woolston
  978-1-925536-88-1 (paperback) 978-1-925536-89-8 (eBook)
- *Filthy Sucre* by Nod Ghosh
  978-1-925536-92-8 (paperback) 978-1-925536-93-5 (eBook)
- *The Story of the Milkman* by Alan Walowitz
  978-1-925536-76-8 (paperback) 978-1-925536-77-5 (eBook)

 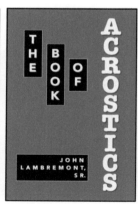 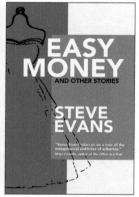

- *Minotaur and Other Stories* by Salvatore Difalco
  978-1-925536-79-9 (paperback) 978-1-925536-80-5 (eBook)
- *The Book of Acrostics* by John Lambremont, Sr.
  978-1-925536-52-2 (paperback) 978-1-925536-53-9 (eBook)
- *Easy Money* by Steve Evans
  978-1-925536-81-2 (paperback) 978-1-925536-82-9 (eBook)

Also from TRUTH SERUM PRESS

truthserumpress.net/catalogue

 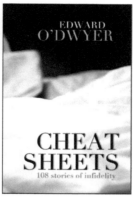 

- *Square Pegs* by Rob Walker
  978-1-925536-62-1 (paperback) 978-1-925536-63-8 (eBook)
- *Cheat Sheets* by Edward O'Dwyer
  978-1-925536-60-7 (paperback) 978-1-925536-61-4 (eBook)
- *The Crazed Wind* by Nod Ghosh
  978-1-925536-58-4 (paperback) 978-1-925536-59-1 (eBook)

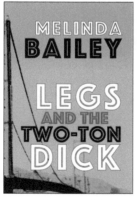  

- *Legs and the Two-Ton Dick* by Melinda Bailey
  978-1-925536-37-9 (paperback) 978-1-925536-38-6 (eBook)
- *Dollhouse Masquerade* by Samuel E. Cole
  978-1-925536-43-0 (paperback) 978-1-925536-44-7 (eBook)
- *Kiss Kiss* by Paul Beckman
  978-1-925536-21-8 (paperback) 978-1-925536-22-5 (eBook)

Also from TRUTH SERUM PRESS

truthserumpress.net/catalogue

- *Inklings* by Irene Buckler
  978-1-925536-41-6 (paperback) 978-1-925536-42-3 (eBook)
- *On the Bitch* by Matt Potter
  978-1-925536-45-4 (paperback) 978-1-925536-46-1 (eBook)
- *Too Much of the Wrong Thing* by Claire Hopple
  978-1-925536-33-1 (paperback) 978-1-925536-34-8 (eBook)

- *Track Tales* by Mercedes Webb-Pullman
  978-1-925536-35-5 (paperback) 978-1-925536-36-2 (eBook)
- *Luck and Other Truths* by Richard Mark Glover
  978-1-925101-77-5 (paperback) 978-1-925536-04-1 (eBook)
- *Hello Berlin!* by Jason S. Andrews
  978-1-925536-11-9 (paperback) 978-1-925536-12-6 (eBook)

Also from TRUTH SERUM PRESS

truthserumpress.net/catalogue

  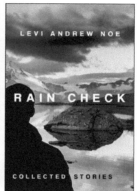

- *Deer Michigan* by Jack C. Buck
  978-1-925536-25-6 (paperback) 978-1-925536-26-3 (eBook)
- *What Came Before* by Gay Degani
  978-1-925536-05-8 (paperback) 978-1-925536-06-5 (eBook)
- *Rain Check* by Levi Andrew Noe
  978-1-925536-09-6 (paperback) 978-1-925536-10-2 (eBook)

  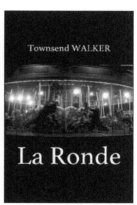

- *Based on True Stories* by Matt Potter
  978-1-925101-75-1 (paperback) 978-1-925101-76-8 (eBook)
- *The Miracle of Small Things* by Guilie Castillo Oriard
  978-1-925101-73-7 (paperback) 978-1-925101-74-4 (eBook)
- *La Ronde* by Townsend Walker
  978-1-925101-64-5 (paperback) 978-1-925101-65-2 (eBook)

from EVERYTIME PRESS

everytimepress.com/everytime-press-catalogue

Travel & Memoir

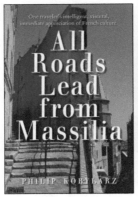 

- *All Roads Lead from Massilia* by Philip Kobylarz
  978-1-925536-27-0 (paperback) 978-1-925536-28-7 (eBook)
- *Lenin's Asylum* by A. A. Weiss
  978-1-925536-50-8 (paperback) 978-1-925536-51-5 (eBook)

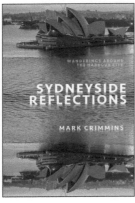  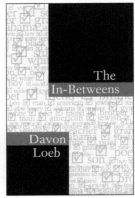

- *Sydneyside Reflections* by Mark Crimmins
  978-1-925536-07-2 (paperback) 978-1-925536-08-9 (eBook)
- *Perro Callejero (Stray Dog)* by Darren Howman
  978-1-925536-96-6 (paperback) 978-1-925536-97-3 (eBook)
- *The In-Betweens* by Davon Loeb
  978-1-925536-56-0 (paperback) 978-1-925536-57-7 (eBook)

from EVERYTIME PRESS

everytimepress.com/everytime-press-catalogue

Resource and How-To books

 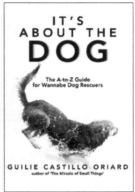

- *The Pointless Revolution!* by Paul Ransom
  978-1-925536-74-4 (paperback) 978-1-925536-75-1 (eBook)
- *It's About the Dog* by Guilie Castillo Oriard
  978-1-925536-19-5 (paperback) 978-1-925536-20-1 (eBook)

- *all you need is a whiteboard, a marker and this book!*
  by Matt Potter (available in paperback only)
  978-1-925536-27-0 (Book 1) 978-1-925536-28-7 (Book 2)

from PURE SLUSH BOOKS

pureslush.com/store

- *The Shitlist Pure Slush Vol. 16*
  978-1-925536-90-4 (paperback) 978-1-925536-91-1 (eBook)
- *Lust 7 Deadly Sins Vol. 1*
  978-1-925536-47-8 (paperback) 978-1-925536-48-5 (eBook)
- *Gluttony 7 Deadly Sins Vol. 2*
  978-1-925536-54-6 (paperback) 978-1-925536-55-3 (eBook)

 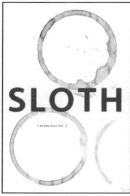 

- *Greed 7 Deadly Sins Vol. 3*
  978-1-925536-64-5 (paperback) 978-1-925536-65-2 (eBook)
- *Sloth 7 Deadly Sins Vol. 4*
  978-1-925536-66-9 (paperback) 978-1-925536-67-6 (eBook)
- *Wrath 7 Deadly Sins Vol. 5*
  978-1-925536-68-3 (paperback) 978-1-925536-69-0 (eBook)

from PURE SLUSH BOOKS

pureslush.com/store

 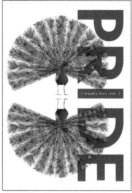 

- *Envy 7 Deadly Sins Vol. 6*
  978-1-925536-70-6 (paperback) 978-1-925536-71-3 (eBook)
- *Pride 7 Deadly Sins Vol. 7*
  978-1-925536-72-0 (paperback) 978-1-925536-73-7 (eBook)
- *Happy² Pure Slush Vol. 15*
  978-1-925536-39-3 (paperback) 978-1-925536-40-9 (eBook)

  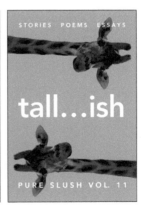

- *Inane Pure Slush Vol. 14*
  978-1-925536-17-1 (paperback) 978-1-925536-18-8 (eBook)
- *Summer Pure Slush Vol. 12*
  978-1-925536-13-3 (paperback) 978-1-925536-14-0 (eBook)
- *tall…ish Pure Slush Vol. 11*
  978-1-925101-80-5 (paperback) 978-1-925101-98-0 (eBook)